I0145371

UNTIMELY LIGHTENINGS

Untimely Lightenings

BEING POEMS AGAIN

by
ANNA RIST

Angelico Press

First published in the USA
by Angelico Press 2023
Copyright © Anna Rist 2023

All rights reserved:
No part of this book may be reproduced or transmitted,
in any form or by any means, without permission

For information, address:
Angelico Press, Ltd.
169 Monitor St.
Brooklyn, NY 11222
www.angelicopress.com

ppr 978-1-62138-910-1
cloth 978-1-62138-911-8

Book and cover design
by Michael Schrauzer

In grateful memory of my parents,
Sidney and Thérèse Vogler,
who early encouraged
my love of poetry.

CONTENTS

Thanks are due to Adrian Brink of Lutterworth Press for allowing the re-publication (with slight emendations) of 'Redeunt Saturnia Regna' and 'Autostrada', which first appeared in my *We Etruscans*.

Untimely Lightenings

BEING POEMS AGAIN

GRANTCHESTER MEADOWS IN JUNE

A sandal-squelch reminds us rain
fell heavily in May; still in the main
on dried crazed mudcake we pad
athwart the meadow; varieties of
graminous heads thigh-high
hide the river till its snaking's
sudden seen where coarser grasses
flattened to footpath offer picknickers
purchase to offload from punts
pole-pinioned in the flaccid flow:
scope too for couples impetuous
as once were we, and now, please God,
only subdued to wiser loving.
Reserved to us one final niche
where to seat us, welcome sun's
frontal fondle, outstretch feet
toward the slow stream that's ours
as is none other: Cam, who here
presents his quiet surface quiver
punctuate by plop of fish
or random dart of dragon blue...
Until heaves into hearing
Voice declaiming, presaging
punt-pole pulling into view
punctuating her recital
girl delivering to companions
poet dead in lines familiar
to triteness—but not trite her zeal
nor for mocking. We listen as
her treble round each fenny bend
returns acute to the last
well-known syllable. We say nothing
each, we know, remembering
the multitudes Cam has borne young
and poets grown not old...

I

LONDONERS

I was born in a City of Martyrs
and suckled at her niggard breast
of parents each proud of a birth-right
he from East of the City, she West.
And Londoners born or new out of
the Midlands were grandparents three
the fourth intermarrying Krakow's
fair city oppressing oppressed.

Hazard he'd undertake for a Freedom
known fickle: would fleeing enlist
for her maintenance in the old City
new-smoking since risen afresh
from under her first fire-fed pall:
there to work there to rise there die
eluding more fell fires than would fall
on streets he'd bequeath to his seed.

City till late by blanketing fogs
poisoned in alleys man-trapping:
in littering stews clap-trapped
worser than fog or fire burden!
O London, City of Martyrs and
Krakow, giver of saint to illumine
our times: even as Vistula merged
in Thames, stream this blood on ...

CORPUS CHRISTI

Now I'm an old woman, at last I can be
that person who underneath always was me

though from youth onward ever oppressed
by how to appear, doubtful how to be dressed:

how not to be noticed as notably odd—
least of all by provoking the question of God:

for religion may pass for funerals and Sundays
but should be laid aside for working- and fun-days—

with particular care lest at parties and dinners
in your cups you offend by remarking on sinners...

And so has life passed, until sudden one's eighty
and life-and-death questions begin to loom weighty

though what they come down to is: given I seem
to exist—unless that's in Somebody's dream—

and through no choice of mine, all I can decide:
is either keep going or commit suicide

that unresolved person who may prove to fit me
not to pursue to the end seems a pity—

So!

I can sport fuddy hats; I don't have to wear bras;
I can tootle around in far-from-smart cars;

I won't have a face-lift or boob-job: such action
is bound to end up in dissatisfaction—

So!

I'll eschew what's now the national cult of shopping
clump in comfy shoes however clod-hopping

3

not bother powdering my nose. No!
This little light of mine,
let it shine, shine! Shine...

So!

I'll wear a crucifix or a medal: show
me still the same child the Father will know.

SEASCAPE

Bid me fare well
faraway sea
I, island child, early loved you:
strove in your surges swim
bestrode you on billowed decks
souther thrusting from our clime.

Late I look back
our parting past
save where veiling shifts of mist
glimpsed through driven screen
signal you subsist
greatest treasure for Earth made!

Sea-strand, sea-shaped
sea-soon-to-wrack
thought to breaking sound subduing:
planted and on this shelf
jetsam-like upheaved
after long living overseas

might we restart
synchronical
each heart for tranquil ending
interlocked contritions
scissor weedy tangles
uncovering submerged shoals:

each cape landmark
our ebbtide motion
as rocks sea-tossed are grounded
toward gulf shall cast us last
ashore where knowledge is
and number of each grain of sand.

SORT OF SONNET

Streaming Crete-ward in a thunderstorm
waves whelming over deck: we on it
clinging persistent to avoid peasants
vomiting below and in despite of
groanings holding onto trussed feet
of chickens sequin-eyed staring upward.

Steaming into the lagoon-womb
Of Venice after a night on deck steady
enough to be shared with the Greek army;
waking I fling off one conscripted arm:
lonesome I conclude, not meaning harm
just dreaming he's back home with his girl . . .

You can't make such voyages now: all's
cruise-boats like floating shopping-malls.

O!

O wild Welsh weather!
O lowering clouds counting
out raindrops on my windshield!
O lifting of lowering vapours
from shaley hillsides
scabrous, grey-green!
O wandering walls
and walls compact!
O snaking stream,
Grey lake!
O purpling spires of
drifted foxgloves!
O patient sheep, that show us
how to be mothers!
O wringing of their wool-knit gifts
and spreading in hope to dry as
we drift into rain-pelted sleep...

SONNET IN PISCIFORM

Sister, far up some sun-simmered sound
our flesh at spawning fell; a mild tide
caught and carried us and soon we found
mouths had only to open blindly wide
and nourishment came nuzzling, sifted
by silent sands, blent in a glaucous glow
becalmed our questing sense, and so we drifted
sight unripe: whereto we could not know.

until a coldness plucked at us, a pit
foundered below as shelved our world away.
In skeleton and skull and wrack the writ
disclosed was to be preyed on or to prey.
That fulcral moment I became aware.
I turned and for a first time knew you there...
    . . .
(alternate sestet):
till that moment I became aware
the bottom of our world had shelved away:
a cold below swell pulling back
picking at skeletons, humping wrack
niggard of life gave each to each as prey.
I turned and for the first time know you there...

8

MOONSET

(As herein implied, poem was
composed before the moon-landings.)

(*Strophe*)
There you are, Moon, much as a week ago
except that then your other edge was rubbed
and you preparing your sleek full-waxed
stare at us passers-by in the betweenings
of flat-black'd roofs and chimney-stacks...
Or if we streets quit and sought the meadow
as though by you the ribbon-river ran
silvered with willow-silhouettes' wet leanings
and poplar shapes cut out to prop a show
all yours, you the more enthroned and queening...
Say, Moon, do you remember two whose sight
in one other's seeming seemed your light:
nor one's nor your nor third's but eye of being
full-blown and bodying with all
that born grows to the full fades to the wane
dies and is born again? Of you how strange
we spoke, how seemingly elusive you
hang and spite of rocket-reach unmanned
remain our Moon of Heraclitean change...

(*Antistrophe*)
Selene quo me rapis tui plenam?
Let me not so speak as though I were
child of primal wrath, some devotee
of Ashtaroth or Hellene worshipper
of all the light he knew. The roundel raised
between men's hands is my God, not you!
When will you cease to draw inert the minded
even as tide draws into the sand?
True lunatics we the moon-blinded
while you the used to mark the menses and
nine womb-months are super-woman'd:
no more, Artemis, blood your claim—

9

though Archetype perchance be made your name—
and Moon you soon, your crescent Muse decreased
to mind-size measured shall be manned,
Science troth keeping with Faith to end
your maiden-maddening reign! Then One
shall deliver you our gain and sign
distinguishing the hand of the High Priest.

AUTOSTRADA

(First appeared in We Etruscans,
Lutterworth 2000.)

Car underdrowned in wavering pitch
fumed from slag-mash compound which
careers beneath the axles' ride
carrier buckled by bolt and solder
glass and metal two-way ranked
side by side to side and flanked
by no-man's-lane, a sterile shoulder
nor any between but paint to divide
steel from steel and the plushy seat
offering shrivelling nerves retreat...

Reeling kilometres broken
by turrets where scant word is spoken
and hardly human form imprisoned:
in each a minion corpse soul-wizened
hand a handle to take a ticket
automatical to stick it
in a slot brainboxed assesses
myriad lire accrued between
hand that recoils and hand that presses
soundless changes of red and green...

Powers alongside surging send you
trumpeted vibes *diminuendo*
to vanishing point; the "extra long"
articulated lorry's song
swells with howls of a hundred hells;
clutch down haul past straining shells
abdomen thorax cabhead, the core
a tanned jaw glimpsed, a muscular paw
of a stolid trucker set in motion
to plough a continent like an ocean...

Count down brake down signal filter
steering keeping wheels a-kilter
crawling peering craving space
on a parkless pullulant surface
whence even the wretched weeds have fled
leaving the dead disgorge their dead.
Wind up lock up stow under seat
cash cards cameras; can you defeat
the fable-fingered Napolitano
may lurk even in Val d'Arno?

Servizi—decidedly not what they were since
Mercedes-riders, merciless race
of brand-new knights, have reversed warfare
rationalizing the old *Kultur-*
kampf for a Europe *in Ordnung*, pure
of the cheerful neo-roman mess
possessing life as a wilderness
to be muddled through by good God's grace.
Now plate-glass foursquare inward entices
posting depictions of packaged ices...

or outside if you're spry you'll get a
patch of scrub where a single zany
thorn-bush casts mean shade and many
before you have left their *sigaretta-*
butts and *carta di toiletta*;
the houseflies flock to it: still better
than bar's or car's close-closeted
halitoses, than concreted
hardstanding exusting* drouth
to shrivel a picnic, wrap to mouth...

---

*   I hold myself licensed to coin this word.

Back on tarmac there's been planned a
meandering line of oleander
resisting grit and sear of sky
oasis to the dust-worn eye
their sheaved-in-green marshmallows deck
the median yet not quite conceals
a companion barrier of steel's
onward march in hope to check
the not-so-young peninsular male
proving his manhood on your tail . . .

Still pigeon-passions point our car
sun's way balked of a homing line
by a tuckering fringe of the Apennine
till Siena foregone and Firenze afar
Amiata's chestnut mane the comb
of Labbro departs to sign us home.
By hamlet-steadings our hill-crook'd way
sallies on down remaindering day
till Fiora's freshets Albegna's chills
enfold us last fast in the travertine hills.

TRESPASS

(*Runner-up, Manchester Cathedral Poetry Competition*)

When God designed a garden
paradise for man,
a hostile bid was entertained.
So trespassing began.

Then Eve took fruit for Adam,
Cain took his brother's life,
Noah took to drink, King David
took to Uriah's wife.

God kept making comebacks
till Judas shopped the friend
Peter denied and Paul pursued
beyond the bitter end.

These two would gain a living
from selling futures: Who'd
be quit of debt, let them acquit
their debtors! Belial chewed

on bile at seeing sinners
make capital of sin.
"To hell with gilt securities!
I'll make you partners in

my brands—all saints! Monsanto
and Fininvest! I'll lay
out sweeteners for Chiquitas—merge,
say, Dessault with BA!

My hirelings all are chartered,
insuring you're not conned.
Trust us! We're in the business of
delivering on our bond!"

SERMO-SONNET

The children of the pharisees
count the minutes on their knees,
count their prayers by their beads,
calculate their least misdeeds
telling by a scruple's weight
how much pain must compensate ...

The children of the Promise know
the dusty stock from which they grow
the fruit of earth it bore and how
the gardener came to break the bough:
so grafted on a nobler tree
they drink the sap humility
nourished by which blessing balm
the driest branch may bear a palm.

LIBERI

(Strophe)
Cornelia bid of her Lord Scipio
produce her jewels brought to him their sons
—or was it children? *Liberi* in Latin
is genderless; nonetheless I'd guess
daughters omitted, they by no personal name
being distinguished, all Cornelias and
told by number: Prima, Secunda, Tertia
et ceterae. Be that as may, Cornelia
presented as her jewels their *liberos:*
it made an improving story for Titus Livius
to illustrate a Roman contempt for show
of no doubt pricey baubles (The Scipios
were gentlefolk and top of the pecking order)
together with exaltation of manly prowess
as magistrate, conqueror—at very least
soldier: in such service of the State
would rest her sons' distinction ... Yet Cornelia
by mother-wit attributes to them worth
transcending mere utility: not tools
but jewels the most prized of her adornments.

(Antistrophe)
As so are you, my four, my jewels in pledge
of immortality: and hence have I
knowing our frailty, daily sued to view
manhood of two, womanhood of two:
so as, God sparing, you to ripeness grew
have with your father measure received
overflowing, being in despite of
distances by you accompanied
into our haler age, while you mature
from taught to teachers: become handers-on
of virtue as of knowledge, grace on grace.
Scarce born a grandchild and her father's
life threatened, was orphaning spared, hearts'

pleas heard. Second and third time Satan
enraged at sacrifice—which holy-making
means—and setting-apart of firstborn's firstborn
struck at our line in vain—and if again
may God forfend, Who rather has our house
inset into a lordly brotherhood*
one gem in one encircling diadem.

* The Dominican Order of which our eldest grandson is now a
priest-friar.

RING

O ring
worn thin
on my finger
long time since
before altar
by bridegroom
for wedding
there placed
nor birth-giving
nor I otherwise
anaesthetised
removed but care-taped
there by nurse smiling

o ring!

O ring
bride-vow sealing
wear we together
till from this hand
from this-world grapple
years more than half an
hundred and counting
away you are drawn and
to next-of-kin given
else intact in coffin for
age-after unearthing
or Doom me waking
unworn you wearing

o ring!

DRESSING-GOWN

You little valued it the day she placed it
on your then single bed beside the socks
shirts slippers, kit she'd purchased for you
an expensive-looking silk dressing-gown
paisley-over-patterned in a ruby red
shot through with peacock blue:
what use, you thought, to you
an Essex boy scornful of such fusses
and have worn at most six times in sixty years
—yet the silk threads threaten come apart
around the armhole where now I stitch it . . .

It crowned the other clothes, was of her choosing
after your father had you suited twice
for day and dinner; both desired their sinner
should cut it as a gent, so gladly spent
out of the winnings of a thrifty life.
Thus your parents at parting forward looking
as backward now your then-future wife
surveying a scant lifetime following
over mountains between continents
her portioned destiny and seeming reason
for being, I here sit stitching on

her gift: your mother's, proud her only son
was for the Varsity—to study what
no matter: she'd dress him like the gentleman
she'd dreamed he'd be, though that provoked his scorn
and he to nobler aims would make his claim.
You left, crossed an ocean, wed, got children
even made something of a name . . .
Her latest word was 'Nothing matters now'
and I, as I sit stitching in our twained
life's waning fain would from me ward
thought of her providing for your shroud . . .

CHILD IN PLANE

Child who in plane
travel airily from me
who not to my bane
speed your way on
anxieties beguiled
in specious loquacity:
shall years again
bring you to make of me
in eld your child:
bring on that day
that let of none other
we in our frailty
stay one another
so travel slow on
toward dissolution
to world not in vain
and heavenward our gain?

FIFTY

My babe you are fifty
yet still babe to me
albeit I prayed
to see you man grown
having thrice stood
to lose you: in womb
threated and birthing
nutrient cord
tightened to throttling...
Last through self-love
and care-lack: by kind
—so pleased it God—
endeavour reclaimed...

Yet through all years
between and on
my to eternity babe!

SONS

They flit in and out of our lives
do sons; there's anticipation
that's half the happiness: he's coming
Peter—or Tom—my stalwart tall
babes I grew and though of wives
possessed now many a year my yet
and ever boys.   Their father's glad
to see 'em even if critical
anticipating political
arguments dissents
world set to rights.   I merely want
to admire them anxious to assess
they're fit and healthy
though nearing or past fifty—
God be praised—and modestly successful
in paths they follow: not
that ever they'll be rich
in this-world sense but—God again
be thanked—they've enough of pelf
for some determination of self
and their priorities.
                                    I can't expect
to see them much or long—and each is gone
before you can take your full
draught of the cup.   Daughters stay in touch
but sons flit in and out again
and I am old and this or next time
may be the last—but love brings hope
if they, if I, keep walking straight
up to the line by good God's grace
beyond will lie a mother's shared
consolation passing on
to children of their own
that growing still or grown
pre-occupy them now their wives
are mothers.   Thus their lives

22

mirror ours—as shall their sons'
and theirs through generations
be our precious lending
from now and to world ending.

GIRLS

There used to be such a thing as girlhood
(God be praised!) but now it seems
girls jump toddler to teen, the between
child reaching for its fate
as fearful coupling come too late...

Where are you now, girls that I knew
grave friend Debbie
merry friend Ann
first friend Deb and faithful Ann!

Deb, hardy in hard winter—
that long winter of '47
coal rationed we'd crouch
hands toward poked-up flames:
Deb trudging to school in plimsolls
up Frith Lane past the barracks
sentries unmoving, safe: our Tommies!
'Debbie, you Spartan!' So her class-
master greets her and I'm impressed
both by Deb and by Spartans.
My shoes were leather for I had only
a pair of siblings while Deb had three
and their father drove a bus—a trolley
as Deb insisted—surely secure in
his hands for distinction clung to the tall
ex-Guardsman—and to Deb's mother
that black-haired blue-eyed Celt of Killarney
another kind of distinction.   She a Catholic
had captivated Jack a Proddy:
couldn't have happened where he came from
but they were safe in England; this I
did not then understand just knew
I was welcome in their Council home
with sometimes my brother much of an age
with madcap Johnny whom secretly

I admired. The death he eluded
falling from trees would catch up
with Johnny in the Fleet Air Arm
failing to land his plane on the carrier deck ...
'Paddy', a younger brother
would die of cancer. Poor Deb,
poor family, both brothers,
both sons lost young!

And Deb's
mild beauty, if by sun
over-freckled, was photo-fixed
on their living-room wall, coloured
as if painted: the innocent-eyed
child still blonde. (Later she'd jest,
'My hair's pure mouse!')
                                        Coming
Christmas, Deb and I'd go caroling
with her accordion (treble only;
she'd say she'd learn the bass but somehow
never did): just we two;
our brothers declined when promise of pelf
proved a pittance—and part agreed
for charity I hope was duly
paid, but it never amounted to much ...

After Deb went to the Convent
—where the bus-driver's daughter
from the Council house kept well
her end up with the Spanish princess
who showed them how to pierce their ears
in the dormitory safely—
I who longed to go too
having absorbed convent-school
tales our aunts told before the
fire at Christmas slightly sozzled

(apart from tea-addict Gay—
'short' for Gabrielle and no-one
in those innocent post-War times
would think to snigger) of their schooldays
and 'Mother Harper', a nun to whom
were attributed never too unseemly
pranks involving the Bishop—I
was sent to the Girls' Grammar: both of us
'on the scholarship'.   We still
could holiday together at
my Aunt Mary's in Sussex;   once
we walked the Downs, crossed into Wight
for an island adventure but our lien
stretching ever more tenuous...

Where are you now,
girls that I knew:
first friend Deb
and merry Ann!

Six or eight white ankle-socks
oscillant over the grassed edge
of a superannuated bomb-shelter
tip legs of unequal length.   You said
'My mother told me I was unwanted'
and a new world opens: You?   My friend?
Unwanted?   Later I learned your father
consoled himself this superfluous
daughter might in beauty elegance
fashion do him credit in circles
he cultivated.   They had you trained
in elocution, likely aid
to such distinction: an actress maybe
—anyway star.   Well, star you were
though unfulfilling of his fancy when
you failed to grow upward womanly

developing on stunted legs.
Tried were new hormones: too
late said the doctors. Your mother
outward optimist did she sorrow
taking up huge hems in hope
to let them down again, providing
care for the ungainly child
unloved of the father? (School past
and its uniform, still you'd be buying
child-sizes, whatever would fit
and a fig for fashion!) In compensation
you nurtured a different sophistication
leading us your small coterie
to delight in books art theatre.
On desk-inspections your raised lid
displayed play-reviews postcards
of Rembrandts and for pin-ups Olivier
('Larry' to you) or Gielgud whose voice
thrilled your elocuted ear.
So too the contralto of Miss C. our
English teacher unleashed a 'crush':
what time too our French Miss L
—decidedly not to be styled 'Mamzelle'
albeit her war cry to 'Think in French!'—
called me to her desk to warn
of this *amitié dangereuse*:
likewise my mother apprised by yours
in a phone heart-to-heart competing
doubtless in trials of daughter-rearing
how you had tried to throw your father
downstairs. Really? That tall man
with your pigmy strength? Was it that waked
his vengeance to refuse to pay
for University? Well and who
among us is sinless? I only knew
that where you were things were gay

27

(again as before that word's perversion).
You saw no point in being downhearted
and at length would marry to spend with Frank
librarian lives in companionate reading:
bouts of quiet broken by your
loquacity and his dry
tolerant echo. You bore no child
but made him a comfortable almost
childlike wife: two kindred
souls in tandem till debility
overtaking you ended in death.
We your friends had gone our ways.
Frank lived widowed on: of late
his funeral brings you both in mind.
Your mother, that well-meaning woman —
are you with her now? You ever
declared, 'I'm not religious' — to follow
with a 'but...' You'd dodge school prayers
yet confess to a favourite hymn:
'My Song is Love Unknown'. And given
Love, how much shall be forgiven...

Where are you now
girls that I knew?
Deb, shall we go caroling
on the doorstep of the King?
Ann, may we round Shepherd's Fold
traipse the meadows as of old?

JANE

Our mother told me of your birth:
'our mother' say I though she rather
to my brother, full legitimate
heir might more mother seem
than to me untimely launched
into being reminder of precepts
she must hold transgressed.   Then did
my conception reconcile
my grandfather her father to
her lighting on a Jew to marry?
Chances were few—three of five
daughters would remain unwed
what with toll of War and his
own misfortunes culminating
in death of sole surviving son:
grieving which, 'Another girl!'
he greeted me.   Years three
would barely pass before on world
teetering toward War's renewal
born the desired male—to be
both circumcised and christened.
And War was all but won when comes
word to our Warwickshire retreat
from Jack our father's twin his wife
of a girl brought to bed: the birth
was hard and Doris would not bear
again: this the reward of Hebrew
faithfulness: the cast-off twin
going on to sire a male
upon his *shicksa* wife...   She
already seizing on occasion
to demonstrate sisterly joy
had set eight-year-old me
to knitting baby bootees in
an aquamarine tint suited
to either sex.   Alas, the gift

fell short with Jack complaining
—rightly it may be—we failed
to enquire after Doris.   Years
would pass before in constrained visits
we cousins met but at my wedding
they were present with Jack making
note of rooms and costs—my father
had struck a Jewish bargain to follow
the marrying in self-same church
where he and my mother adjusted had
their knot (She stressed she had worn purple;
it would appear my bridal white
irked her—but that's another story).
I went overseas and years
would pass before we cousins again
met with Jane poised to home
over ocean from trip designed
to marry her into Jewish praxis.
But Jane you never would give them the hoped-for
heir: they died grandchildless
and you would follow single to
your end: did you then fear
Jewish matriarchy though still
in some sort wedded to their Faith?
You to your hunched little mother
were the good daughter, attentive
loving better than I to mine.
Now in the Jewish cemetery
your grave makes third to theirs.
I saw you last a hospice patient
facing death though seeming still
your carefree self.   And Death would come
to cut you off even as might
confidence seem betwixt us building.
With my mother can I hope
in heaven to have understanding

father entrust to Rabbi Paul's
dictum that the unbelieving
husband by the believing wife
is sanctified. Then shall I sorrow
for leaving you unsteered toward
baptism when occasion might
seem to offer—or ask myself
to what end professions of
piety if you in some
anteroom to heaven languish
through my lack?
    Then, Jesus
Your pardon on me and on Jane
Your mercy that we meet again...

TRUTH

I guess you were a silly girl, not only in
the trivial sense we give that word that comes
from 'seel' meaning soul, hence innocent
as soul new-Christ-washed in baptism:
as was yours and after you came to years
of understanding when lost is innocence
you made First Communion: there's a photo—
sepia but your veil shows weighty white
enough to have satisfied that prophet who
it seems had a penchant for young girls:
(*penchant* in French meaning 'inclination'
docked of its final 'n' is Latin; but
and in whatever tongue, our inclinations
—word implying a tending downward—need
resisting.)
                    Well and to resume: I was
innocent after you had me laved of
our forefathers' sin, when you gave pains
I'd not grow a silly girl; instead
I grew a serious and began to question
things you'd have me believe but I found wide
of truth. (Of course what I call truth will not
stand up merely because I hold it but only
implying a Truth objective, 'out of this world'
and yet relating to it.)   I would revert
to Truths you had been taught but part rejected
for what seemed, seems a compromise
but Truth must judge.   Opportunities
you had lacked opened to move me on.
You'd have liked to have me near, attendant
on your age as you with sisters hovered
attendant on your Mother: she the more
than mother to me as I grew oft dismayed
(the which observing one among that band
exact in faithful dealing would confide
you 'always preferred men'.)

I was I know
a disappointing daughter but Day comes
shall purge away in Truth's blaze all
misunderstanding and we stand before
God's own Mother mothers and reconciled . . .

MELANCHOLY
(*All Souls 2016*)

Two brothers I have
and soon the one
his lifeline spun
death shall have won.

Two sons I have
and they are stol'n
from out the land
and to two brides gone.

Two daughters I have
and each makes moan
her narrow way's
with brambles strown.

Husband I have
that is mine own
till death-undone
one left is lone.

Then Spirit come
with Father Son
us to atone
and make your own...

NOT VALE

Brother, I do not say with the poet of his
beloved almost-island Sirmio
'Hail and farewell!': poet trammelled in toils
of a politic mistress, shunning the Rome of her
turbulent brother stirrer of revolution
with dagger and what weapons a populace
may wield. Of him, Clodius of the Claudii
plebbing it with that clipped vowel, we know
much—as that the poet and his brother
were heritors likewise of an ancient name
the 'little whelps', the Catulli. Of the brother
we know only what our poet tells us:
that he died and they raised his pyre upon a sliver
of land betwixt two waters: Sirmio
or in the oblique successor tongue, Sirmione.

So in contemplation of loss the poet
seeks consolation. Of you my brother
after your year's inexorable decline
for me emerges a photograph—black and white
fixing the war-strapped 'fifties in the boy
who looks to camera, collar and tie correct   (if
the latter a little askew) above a crested
blazer: already he seems to pose question
a public-school faith won't answer—though
its Master a cleric, impressing parents and even
haply beneath their callow jeering the boys . . .
Meanwhile War's panoply boosts a Faith
to which boy may subscribe and seems Science
—after a life of conventional church-going
followed by your year's inexorable decline—
all the religion to which you subscribe—literally
imposing to be read at funeral by
the son to whom it has fallen to work your coffin
ecologically with no nails
your testament to incredulity.

Yet not for you modernity's gas-fired
version of the pyre; for you a hole is
dug high up on the distant windswept moorland.

And yet Science—meaning Knowledge, *Scientia*—
tells of a world of an intricacy seems
infinite and to marvel at: of a God
perforce the Beyond-Science—nothing of Him
(Her if it please you: no pronoun ties down God:
this Julian, first recording authoress
of English, understood, invoking a Her
as Mother): nothing of God can mankind
(term inclusive, however the pure may cavil)
apprehend unless in contemplation
of *Scientia*'s subjects, done away
all anthropomorphising (Unless,
Thomas will add, by special revelation).
So a *via negativa* holds
reflecting man as in a mirror inverted
and proceeds analogical
from Unbegotten through First-begotten Word . . .

Brother, from that northern country where
you lie, our ancestor departed changing
(So he put it) cut of his coat back
to his forebears' fashion, and being duly disowned
took out of Burgundy a Catholic bride:
thence with irreligions inverted returned
to marry a daughter into an English stock
clinging to Catholic recusancy down to
our mother's generation.

                              So I as I cast
on your coffin earth and hear it 'Dust-to-dust'
sputter pity your stonier path and pray
the One who portioned you this purgatorial
year's slippage to the death that waits
on Everyman grant your store laid up
of good deeds merit our re-meeting.

TO JONATHAN MY BROTHER

("He is now!": response of a Dominican novice
to being told "He was not religious.")

(Strophe)
You did not know the import of that day,
Candlemas, when after slow decline
your candle's flame—was it with final
flicker?—went out. "Sleep in the peace
of Christ" reads your memorial on
this returning Feast, "and with the sign
of Faith." You had taken pains to leave
your testament to non-faith to be read
at funeral by your son: this your planned
ending—but did God see otherwise?
"*Dis aliter visum*" wrote the pagan
of a certain Christian intuition (This
Dante understood making Virgil
his heavenward guide); and did you having left
your declaration of unbelief to be read
at funeral by your son, let go, suffer
a ray from boyhood light up evensongs
and matins you'd walk surpliced in procession
pride of our mother who from stricter bonds
turned to pastures she deemed green—but seems
to you unmeshed from her barren become?

(Antistrophe)
Yet that you fell last into a Father's
hands I hold signaled by this Day
that dawned on you freed from flesh's failure
and pained struggle: being the Day of Christ's
Presentation in the Temple, there
to be proclaimed by ancient prophetess
whose name descended to the still small sister
invited peer into the hooded cradle
whose dark conceals where you lie newborn
new-circumcised yet to be christened.

37

So we by Providence of Him that wills
no lamb be lost for lack of going after
and seeking through whatever Christ-cross'd ways,
surety have and faith that though on earth
at odds, we yet shall stand as reconciled:
this my solace as Mass of your memorial
opens on that Temple where's proclaimed
salvation to Gentile as to Jew: that we
shall meet and greet at last in love and mutual
understanding.   And   so, brother,   fare well!
Vale, Frater—et in aeternum Ave!

3RD FEBRUARY, ST. BLAISE

Dead now the tapers
tinged to divinity
yesterday's faces in
flickering foretaste
of unwintering:

dead but for houseling
hand sets them crosswise
thwart our decaying
gullets... Hand closed
unhouseled your eyes...

Of sanctity's blazon
Blasius Bishop goes
crutched witness on:
so on unextinguished
lives martyrdom's blaze.

Lend thence a taper
for wayfaring blind
brother* gone from us
that lighted he find
path of purgation.

* Died on Candlemas; see previous poem.

DEATH-DANCE

(a version)

(Strophe)
Death has dogged me all day:
first in priestly hands
raising Host and Chalice;
next mid headlong crowds
filling trundling trolleys:
has flitted on amid daily
tasks and toys and still.
into the sudden sunshine
of this my April birth-date
Death pursues me dozing
upon a garden chair
suddenly back-lighting
lightning-like a lifetime
spent betwixt continents
travelling travailing
home-building willing
fill my pilgrim role.

(Antistrophe)
Sun-scatter's refracted
in thousand dandelion dials
as we drag responsive feet
through the municipal park
homeward—by now a daughter's
home whose daughters in time
may make them homes and wait
patient for their mother
to ply inveterate feet
park-bench to garden-
chair, while we, our stage-time
ended, sleep (as the phrase is
not) with our mothers!   I only
this and each succeeding
day desire my life be
out-spilled into chalice
up-caught upon paten . . .

HORA VESPERTINA
(another version)

Death, you have dogged me all day:
in face uplift
of priest raising Host and Chalice:
in heedless crowds
flitting through store-departments filling
plastic baskets with paltry toys:

next in this my April birthday's
sudden suns
stunning my dotage dozing in
a garden chair:
and reflected in dandelion-dials
where on a municipal bench

we shall sit preparing ply yet-
responsive feet
homeward we say, though rather to
a daughter's home
whose daughters will in time wait patient as
their mother plies inveterate feet

'twixt park and garden, so on through
generations
while we, as the Good Book puts it, sleep
with our fathers
and likewise our mothers, all 'pushing'
(as mine would say) 'the daisies up'.

And so this and each remaining
till latest day,
be our life offered in the chalice
on the paten
Christ's flesh as bread, His blood in wine
the Cross as sign and what more needs.

SNAPSHOT

Night's a time for prayer—
whoso may stay wakeful—
and for poetry's make—
whoso pray makeful:
for making can pray
and be prayer made:

otherwise is poem
nothing more durable
than shadow of shadows
captured by camera for
counterfeit screening
even as life flits.

Then why seek we fix
the moment's signing
in buddleia bending
purple-tuft finger in
thunder of waters
or suchlike tricks

as played out face to face
and your hair curling white
to mesh with mine gray
like our breathings embrace
while the livelong night
we wait on day.

WARFARE

Tossing the blossom from Washington trees
a sinister breath—so subtle a breeze
enfolding enthralling   enrapturing rolls
from sacked Aleppo's hell-holes

and Damascus of Paul;   makes mourn each mother
of orphaned cots   where the monster Murder
loosened to raven   stalks every street
and the spider Fate spins deceit

to fashion on loom   of delicate death
her Nessus-wrap   of gaseous breath
while bear-like a Beast   snarling protection
from east plots ever extension . . .

If their Allah invoked   as destruction's patron
be deaf to all else   our God we call on
to strengthen our arm   firm resolution
to purge His world of pollution.

Crusader desist   from schismatic folly!
Enlist you, resist   their hegemony
blaspheming deriders   of Three in One.
Rouse up!   Put Paul's armour on.

Scorn you to crave   protective perversity
boding your grave!   From University
from whatever workplace   apprenticed be
to the defence of the City!

ARAB SPRING
(another version of the preceding)

Blowing from downtown
Potomac to Capitol
tossing the blossoms off
Washington trees
one sinister breath
through speakers exuding
a poisonous colluding
rolls gently on down
streets of Aleppo
past walls of Damascus
and destitute making
parents rolls on
orphaning beds as
the monster Murder
smiles from his weft
of lethal deceits and
lumbering Beast
proffers protection
ever more east
plotting extension.

If their Allah invoked
as destruction's patron
be deaf to all else, we
on God call to strengthen
our arms with resolve to
withstand this pollution!
Crutched soldier desist
from schismatic folly:
rather enlist 'gainst
usurped hegemony.
Youth, leave to savour
snuffs of perversity:
reaching for spurious
wanton ascendancy
you tread your graves!

Then bring succour, Lord,
to your people of old:
correct our waywardness
bring lies into Your light
and lead us in Your right!

BLOODBATH

Why does it come now to me
in the morn of the nightmare?
Vimy Ridge, Passchaendale:
passion of those who die
in ditches, in foxholes
(so-called, though only dead
would fox be found in them!)
and on the battle-plain
calling on the mothers
who bore them?   It happened
in her infancy, the
mother who bore me:
Mother, did that over-
shadowing omen toughen
you—as tough you were:
'Tough as an old boot!'
I've heard you say, squaring
up to decline.

                        And now
this Europe, old, dying
new-whelmed by strangers:
may as before befell
of older barbarians
the fresh blood revive her:
replenish though never
replace the blood outpoured...

EXECUTIONS
18.8.2015*

One Eastern morning
they cut off a head—
or so they say for to show
the actual slicing on their video
might be counter-productive.

The head was American.
The slicer-off was British
(sort of): the intention
to send a message that in requiring
Submission, Allah means business!

At the Albert Hall the East-West
Dhivan Orchestra receives
four encores, sending a different
message to those who would ban all music:
'Now try cutting off THIS head!'

* Date of Daniel Barenboim conducting Prom at the Albert Hall.

GRANDSON

I for a space provided with your room
experience its character as cell
removed among rooftops: quality not
envisioned in decision not your own
to dwell in this tall house where you'd
clatter up and down its spiral stairway
distracter of parents patient if perplexed
by you their pride, their football-obsessed star
in time to be attuned to a guitar...

I prop my ageing frame on your sturdy
bed: they always bought for you the best
—draw duvet over knees God be praised
the years have spared, face turned to façade
of blank brick drawing eyes upward
to where is planted a rooftop growth of green:
outlook suggesting high vocation dawning?—
then down—Does the pictured Child there
    reach
from His Mother's arms as He would reach
    from yours?—
to settle last on rows of shelved books
perchance might chronicle a faith's flowering.

Yesterday saw you prostrate before altar
over-cloaked with Dominic's authority:
to whose Toulouse entrained begins today's
progression brings you to affirm lifelong
that pledge.   Yesterday too you treading old
Massilia's streets with mother and with sister
a whelp of the Supplanter hurls obscenity
on them, his hate upon your habit.   You
with the Holy Name made answer: so did
the Almighty use the benighted to confirm
your calling to His Word's predication!

Grandson, my fourscore years as once
Anna's in the Temple, have seen
(as haply you hereafter may)
winnower sift wheat from out
the chaff winds whirl away;
have watched wither a season's tares
while steady between grows green
the corn till garnered to evasion
of end-time conflagration.

Then God be pleased and prayed but after
purging owed and owned shall you
with brethren stand with father mother
sister and all we who here
dimly apprehend your meaning.
Him may it please with further in-faith
fathers to enfold us, with
shepherds of selfsame descent
and fashioned from like flesh.
Amen.

'DOLLAR NOR SHARE
HAVE I NONE'

*(I first sketched this poem in response to an invitation
to read some of my poetry to a gathering of friendly
academics at the Catholic University of America.)*

Oft have I 'Fare well!' said to my homeland,
crossed the seas—not as my great-
grandmother Alice, tossed three weeks
on a wallowing barque till at length steaming
against St Lawrence's resolute streaming...
We but the once took ship for a week's
misery tending creeping-in-harness
firstborn round an emptied pool.
Already you could drone your way
in ever-expanding jetliners
a mere eight hours or nine, infant
secure and mainly asleep in a so-called
skycot—and be in Montreal.
By now and long a grandmother
I think little of taking my seat
belt fastened for take-off, glad
of 'extra legroom', time to read
treat myself to a G and T
nap and awake over your Souther
lands that commend themselves to Freedom—
Freedom: how with might and main
obtained: how with hand and grip
maintained!
                    But we're bound
for the ground with a throttling
roar, and it's Dulles: landing planned
in Virginia, state named for a queen
substituting the banned Queen
of heaven whose name in turn fitly
christened that neighbouring state to where
Baltimore led his band of papists

tossed over ocean in caulked hulls
under sail   And here I arrive
am greeted, whisked in Dean John's car—
Seems you Americans have no longer
time for such mouthfuls as 'automobile'!—
to old Colonel Brook's Land
north of Washington's City: whisked
to that varsity, C. U. A., that for now
is home from home in a sullen England.
For strolling here you can sign yourself
with the Cross and nobody's surprised
no-one offended; can kneel to pray
amid doctors a-making, doctors established
doctors past and undying: all Lent
can follow Christ's Progress to Passion;
in Tabernacle can seemly approach
in Him the effulgent Three in One
giving return in a joy that redounds
in young voices—and if on occasion
strident, back-rebounds to call up
Charity—surely here re-found
where's an actual room for Repentance:
what woman or man can more?   Yet more
abounds: in landscape-labourers' toils
bringing fruition in bloom and blossom;
in trunks varyingly up-
thrusting to branch multi-hung
in the even light: in joying bird
and scampering squirrel; is vesper-rung
from crouched dome cross-crowned . . .

⋆   ⋆   ⋆

Forebears were bold to shape them a byre:
Shepherds, water this Brook-Land fold
that your tuition entrust to shoots
strongly nurtured faith's fruition.

51

REDEUNT SATURNIA REGNA

(*First appeared in* We Etruscans,
Lutterworth 2000; slightly emended.)

Here is mens thought incited
to tell us of early time
saw this hilltop sited
where lava lapped with lime
and thrusting a prodigious tunnel
through rock boiled as it passed,
uncrusted as a funnel
to reservoirs vast
miles below this puny hill,
then waited
till they should fill
from floods, by whom created
creature was none to learn,
but aftertimes deduced a godhead hid
to whom some tongue attributed
the name Saturn.

In gratitude
those fathers named for him this colony
collected round the funnel's rim
where welled to a stone brim
the fire-passed waters,
easy laving for their sons and daughters
who surely and securely
thought the God was good
who cleansed and blessed them in this flood
taking from them ills
plagued other people upon other hills
they'd built their stout
walls cyclopean to keep out.

Etruscans came
inherited the town;
Romans the same

rebuilded as pulled down.
All thought the God was good
whose guerdon gushed up in this flood.
Christian centuries
slipped by them at ease
till came the night they by a fearful crack
alerted all ran out
awakened to their lack
to see remains of reeking mud
sucked, turned turbid
as down a spout
below which now was hid
the erstwhile flood.
Lastly the funnel heaved its depths and lay
drying out in sight of day.

Saturnia wept upon her hill
and called on God and saints until
from the countryside about
next day was heard a noisy rout
in the curved vale Etruscans in their time
named for the crescent moon—
to be translated into Latin soon
(as in Macaulay's rhyme)
and to persist still sooner
as the Valle della Luna.
As lymph from giant boil
exited the flood unbounding
to wash a hillside's shoulder
of all that grew and died to soil
out of that valeside steaming
unstoppable and yet redounding
as if insistent to turn back its streaming
stripping from their matrix tree and boulder
it last collected ran in cooling
rivers to where the Tyrrhenian lay muling.

Centuries of resentment
sapped Saturnian contentment
as children's children counted cost
of old Paradise lost
in favour of their neighbours—
so hardly won is Christian resignation—
until an angel of the modern Lord
Capital, putting heads in mind of the reward
accrues to honest labours
in prudent exploitation
of natural resource, drew up a plan
to tap the sulphurous waters as they ran
prodigally to waste and rear a thermal station
should draw *nouvelle richesse* from many a nation
with benefits beside
should flow back to the town from taming
    of that tide!

Yet happily, though times are liberal,
Mammon's still balked of lording over all
and raging waters need expend their wraths
somewhere however cunningly detained in baths.
Albeit in massage-parlour and gymnasium
first for the shareholder and then the patient
triumphs hydraulic issue in induction
of waters doubly purged: though robed
    priestesses
practise on victims fattened their compresses
their maskings irrigations liposuction
and many a ritual new as well as ancient
and though in discreet boardrooms the Market
    rules:
tapped not grossed the wholesale treasure
in suffocating pools
nowise to be pent—
in eddies engineered

whence waddle off
the sickened spoiled
of wealth of leisure
the wined the beered,
the surfeited on rich
saucings to their pasta
at dieting the more aghast: a
Ferrarelle and a lean sandwich—
tapped not grossed the wholesale treasure
drives on its downward path, its spell unspent.

Below in the vale the motley multitude
drives in on pilgrim quest;
some shamble crabwise heaving flesh
on veined stilts—where, where find rest?—
to flop into some hole under the surge and billow.
Even the briefly agile seek refresh
spirit weary, soul already sore
plunged to the neck and all but nude
as the rock made their pillow.
All leave to play awhile; through every pore
discharge the years' detritus that obstructs
the nasal cavities and other ducts.
They breathe anew and ears to antique thunder,
    eyes
attune to antic vapours' dropless rise,
or childlike smear the medicinal mud
blackly on limbs sun warms. That God they
    bless
who ladles them largesse
in so free flood.

APOCALYPSE 2000

(Composed in response to an invitation by the
then-Prior at Blackfriars, Cambridge, to write a poem
on the group-subject of study, being the Apocalypse)

O royal throne of kings, o kingly breed
now given over to the goddess Greed:
brassy Britannia squatting upon seas   XVII 1,15
of effluent and deathblood slick; disease   XI 6, XVI 3
sickles the seals that sport about her skirt
and pesticide and fertilizer hurt
her ways as footpath hedgerow forest field
are bulldozed—holocaust to higher yield:
as butterflies flowers birds grow rare
and British phlegm's no joke in her exhausted air!

Drunk on the cup of her seductions see   XVII 4
wan mothers ply a desperate lottery
in dooming: whom to carry, suckle, whom
scalpel, suction, stab within the womb
that quickens shrinking limbs only to pain.
The spared shall serve apprenticeship to Gain
and fatten on deceits. Will any fight
the Beast that's fought or worshipped?
                         Saints the sight   XIII 4
of Babylon astounds. Our sleaze and sin   XVII 6
Dread Lamb unbuild and new Jerusalem begin!   XXI 2

WAY OF PURGATION

Now that I look back
on a scant lifetime, how
I have followed blindly
between continents, up
mountain, down fell—I ask
was this my being's reason?
Have I not traced out
my woman's destiny?

Bred in a warring world
as I into conscience woke
seemed within my head
swirled battle . . .   (Ah, parents,
tender with pity your young!
Not enough that you strive
to fill mouths, school in
precept you cannot obey!)

So from and to dismay
seemed morrows to drag me
and out of drugged sleep
into soul's turmoil:
seemed none could uncover
what loss in well of me
gnawed cancrous and late
by inward a cry expressed:

'O God, I have lost it, lost it,
thrown it away, have turned me
from arduous slog-path, from
such talent as You bestowed!
O God, I have all but killed it
not enough serving You
stealing light from Your day:
walking with head held proud!

Mediciner of souls
do not even in Bread of
Your Body dose me despair!
Though in sin conceived
for grace I from your bounty
and fount baptized yet wear
long as lingers this half-
light our entail chain.

Then if this be the promised
trial, you yet willing
I misdoubt lest trial be
annulled: if I may surmise
You ever-gracious saying
'Child, have I not told you
My following would be
a daily setting out?'

—and if surmise withstand
doubt, then I'll not sue
for mitigation: rather
trust that in the willing
bearing is burden raised
by Hand shall open eyes
dead to light on Your
smile at sun's rising.

TOM

"Except as little child
you shall become..."
Now all-a-world has smiled
and thought of Tom
who seeing his father
turn down stair
flings self after
trusting hand to reef
him from the abyss
and lead him where his lief
encumbered by no care
already is
    Who reads his mother's mien
by knock-on-board of knife
translated into viands
beneath almighty hands
and knowing no word of
hunger or of life
sends up a claim
would wing a hand of stone
to rain down bread
and so is fed
    Who nurtured on the dues
of a goodwill
he sips from hour to hour
felt some lack
will wilted face
cast down a-wail
but up as soon
expecting grace
unselfconscious
as a flower
flinging his woe away
as wholly as
toy which stayed his
interest a space

Who when his keep
of strength's all down
and its attack all spent
closed tasselled lids
will plummet silk-hung head
asleep right where he sits...
I ask you saints
your Kingdom come
who enters in its gates
but one like Tom!

CONFESSION

(Strophe)
My confessor suggests—rather than enjoins—
I write a poem; so what write—or better
say? Confession's a literal speaking-out
hence a declaring oneself repentant... As shall
I not be—in understanding how
you from your beginnings took refuge
under a carapace of righteousness:
awarded yourself that medal whose obverse
guilt assigned your uncertain spouse my father
and before-looked-for daughter—me—our rankings?
But not mine to play the accuser: this
the entail of man-woman-kind from her
Eve the Mitochondrial as now
we specify her scientifically.

(Antistrophe)
And so I was born into a world preparing
renewal of war your birth had encountered
but husband-father guiltier grown than Cain
at not having died with Abel, and henceforth
Shoah-barred from baptismal laving. Let me
confess with a 'Bless me, father, for I have failed
in understanding'—and if I but begin
to understand, how thoroughly do You
Father from whom is named all fatherhood!
Then on this day of anniversary
forgive what child's folly, youth's arrogance
failed to discern. Let there be peace upon them
and betwixt us for Your world that comes.
Amen.

> 13. 3. '19   (being the anniversary of both
> my parents' deaths, nineteen years apart)

CLIFTONVILLE

'It's the nicer end of Margate', our mother said.
I wished it had been Margate—a proper seaside
where my Patrol Leader had been: goddess
tall and svelte whose slender ankles I
admired from our upper flat as she stood at the bus-stop.
Well, when War's ending meant we could go
to the fabled seaside—only a week and only
a boarding-house, not a proper hotel—with our young
cousin and aunt (our uncle still in Germany
where he exchanged a single bar of chocolate
for a model train that started a whole railway
filling a room in their house: a cousin unborn
would grow up to work on the real one...)
                                        Well, to resume:
our aunt was fun—no doubt relieved her man
had survived the War—and our Grandad too 'came down'
and being not one to 'do things by halves'
with a shovel borrowed off his landlady
built us a sandcastle moated and large enough
for us to sit in—and I don't doubt
will have gone daily to Mass at St Anne's Church
on the Esplanade: nor that that dedication
will have prompted a prayer to the greatest of grandmothers
for Anna his grand-godchild. I would come
to know that church at a later date. But for now
was born another lifelong passion: the sea!
I set myself to swim with a rubber ring
providentially punctured but seems not thought
hazardous in days that had known hazard.
Longing to take all home with me, I planned
a miniature beach with sand and yes, sea-water,
in a cigarette-tin: a valued item in those
'shortage'-days. (Of course, it leaked!)
                                        We had
ices too, real ice-cream in cones
faintly recalled from 'before The War'. War
had spawned warnings of unexploded munitions

further down the front. these I took
for granted, just the way things were—even if
my smaller brother might seem more unsettled ...

*   *   *

Cliftonville! I would return, a swain
persuading me we'd work in an hotel
he as waiter, I as chambermaid:
ignominy lasting a day or two
till I found a better berth teaching English
to foreigners: there was even a German
—known only as the enemy; she taught me
Goethe's most famous line: '*Verweile doch,
du bist so schön!*' But life would never linger.

And there I met Dora: Gift truly
and one of wayside guerdons, guardians back
to faith of forebears. So as day declined
I'd wend way shoreward—to find myself
passing St Anne's Church: would enter, be
enveloped in Person'd silence inviting stay ...

But ever as sun declined, as Evening Star
rose, my gaze traversed that Estuary
seeking out where one I know subsists
to draw me from across its shimmering tide ...
Two loves beckon: how be reconciled
and how God answer this new agony..?

MINE, SAYS THE LORD

Grand Isle of the South, Australia
you have exulted in your condemnation
of the innocent and in your land
My anointed viceroy.   Hypocrites

pouring out your vials of presumption
on the head of truth and virtue, have you forgotten
the final throw of all earthly games
is mine and cast in favour of restitution?

Thus—and to bring you into a repentance
not without holocaust of bird beast
woman man—I decree you mourning
in no other sackcloth than your ashes.

For see, greed has shrivelled the green spaces
of your leased land and I of lands Lord
have only to discharge my lightning 'gainst
your guilt and folly to set all ablaze...

13TH MARCH

Under my young red maple you stand
if ill-assorted hand in hand
he somewhat to fore: so she'll show
not too noticeably taller. Each's
due smile is camera-frozen, stilled
likewise her hand's tremor, omen of
encroaching quake. As if in compassion
dying leaves strew a ground unstirred
by spook wind or are momently
arrested off-fallen from their likewise
stilled source, my sapling's russet crown.

It was your second visit and this time
by air. You first had come over ocean
arriving full of the joys of the voyage: you'd won
a competition, dined at the Captain's table
(You'd know how to behave: no slurping, no
licking of your knife: misdemeanours
she'd condemn at home). How much tide
has since evaporated between continents
condensed as rain hail snow, as I
recall our new-born first daughter: how
she'd cry and you'd wheel her round the block
to put off feeding-time, taking charge
as I grew agitated and our son
reacted in accordance with his age
('Surely!', a doctor upbraids—we returning
on visit to our native land, 'You surely knew
two years the worst gap between births!')
But neither could your presence reassure
nor exchange of city heat for a too
basic lakeside cabin. You went on trips:
Niagara fulfilled your expectations
Québec not... Well, we survived!

Fast-forward (as they say) few years
and planes have more than literally taken off:
one brings you to meet your latest grandchild
whom photo shows sat on a pony while
his siblings have riding-lessons. You stand beside.
'Push me!' he said and we laughed.

Later you'd wait for me to mention your hand's
tremor and when I did say with bravura
'I'll be pushing the daisies up!' and look
to see how I'd take it. 'Shaky Trakey'
our father called you, attempting tease—but you'd
outlive him by nineteen years to die
on same date—was there meaning in that?
My brother took charge of your cremation, so
you didn't precisely push the daisies up!

Of late comes report my maple still
stands, grown a lofty tree to purge
the city air, while we have wandered homing
in varied places. So on this thirteenth
of March, your anniversary, I light
taper overleft from Candlemas*
before your photo *in memoriam.*

---

* Date now of said brother's death. See p. 39.

TOWN AND GOWN

Long since were clerkly fathers wise
to found in far-off fens a haven
where youth and age and in time even
both sexes might acquire
learning in diverse faculties.
Colleges sprang, gave occupation
and in due course were bicycles
favoured means of transportation—
so cleanly, keeping all so pretty
Cambridge was known as Cycle-City.

Until they built a motorway
From London, named it 'M-Eleven'
presaging the fractious fray
as tourists erst by Oxford bound
for York and Edinburgh found
Cambridge next place to heaven.
First to savage was that street
agelong known as 'Petty Cury'
as Boots and boutiques vied to greet
new profits of commercial fury.

Soon to city's desecration
tourists swarmed from farthest nation
loudly elbowing us aside
crowding cluttering our river
with punts so laden and so wide
as scarce between was seen Cam's quiver
while on periphery located
commercial interests competed
and cyclists traffic-menaced quit the
streets of New Camside Silicon City...

Till lately hath just Providence
as checking the importunance
of nations presuming to prevail

used them for Its very flail
and Covid-angel's flaming sword
warding off th'encroaching bane
with leave to unleash new plagues over
peoples unreadied to recover
hath with travel-bans restored
our streets our town to us again!

M.K.H.

I remember walking by the river
one of those long Cambridge days of sunshine
and endless-seeming youth, beside my friend
as you, handsome, debonair, received
her chatter, lordlily replying as
we returned to college after lectures.
I on her other side neglected third
was largely silent and did not then know
I would come to marry one who would
recall you from your schooldays, when as later
effortlessly you rose from pattern prefect
to 'Head Boy' and on to the 'varsity.
Later you went abroad but would return
to Cambridge to become a leading spirit
in contesting that Christian Faith your school
had aimed to inculcate—it seems preferring
to hold its Foundation Protestant despite
dating to still regnant Mary Queen
when its Catholic Founder* in providing
for boys' education, made what amends
he might for burning of William Hunter, young
defender of the newly Protestant faith.
Yearly the boys processed to church to mark
his witness while to drive the lesson home
stood open in the library for all
to read—if scarcely wholesome—Foxe's Tome.
Returned to Cambridge you held seminars
no Christian might attend, no Protestant
let alone Catholic.   But await the upshot.
Last met with in the Cambridge market by
your erstwhile schoolfellow at the stall
of dead fish, you a week on were dead
while he you encountered there lives on
to counter your profane professions, God
being not ready cancelled: not mocked!

* Sir Anthony Browne

SECOND ANN

You came—almost you transpired—
in this my, our-all wane-time:
a quiet Ann as if replacing
my Ann only death could repress
as she soldiered on from our schooldays.

You, second Ann, were soldier
of different metal: prayer your weapon
and daily faithfulness too briefly
by us beheld before you vanished
from our Sunday post-Mass messing.

Haply our new friendship sweetened
lonesome days drawing to close
unbefriended unbeknown
too late enquired of when your body
dead a fortnight found in bathtub...

So would yours be latest funeral
before lockdown decreed: solitude
you at least were spared. Sparse such
kindred as came—perchance fearful of
pandemic: strangers too to the Mass.

Thus were we your all-new friends
and one friar in spirit kin
sad-'social' distanced in
Church of St Laurence gridiron-martyr
below his stony-imaged gaze:

I there minding both Anns' jetsam
lightly shoulder-borne to slither
into indignity of combustion
the one unchurch'd and one with blessing
sped on to crematorium...

TRAINS

Unimaginably long ago
we sat in a train just we two
at opposite corners of the foursquare
box compartment: small girl
smaller boy playing the train-game.
It was perhaps our parents' suggestion
seeing us on, having arranged for
our uncle to meet us off: those
were trusting times, times of pulling
together to end the War. (It ended
when I was nine, you six.) Or
perhaps it was my suggestion—given
I'd beat you every time at spotting
farm animals: scoring four
for a horse, three for a cow, two
for a sheep (and probably I'd claim
to count a whole flock fast enough!)
Who reached fifty won and so
I'd triumph: small wonder that
we quarrelled! God alone knows if
things might have been different between us.

But now it all seems unimaginably
long ago—and you are dead;
then why do I address you as though
alive? Your parting message—written
in bitterness with instruction it
be read at funeral by your son
was of No Hope. You had striven
to be a public-school pukka
Englishman—living up to our mother's
view of you. Our father too
would have liked to have been pukka-
English and I'd guess was something
of an embarrassment with which
you did not come to terms to embrace
our part-Jewish incorrectitude.

And so I last saw you pitifully lean
half-resenting our presence, refusing
the Communion your wife had arranged
for the vicar to bring you. Then shortly
after, even as dawned the Feast of
Purification, Candlemas
the fast-closing doors of your carriage
slid finally shut and your train
departed, God its destination...

FOR THE RECORD

This house that assembles chance-seeming
fragments of our life is one of
twelve—or is it thirteen? There was
our first married home: a basement
flat or as we learned to call it
'apartment': windows at ground level
number fourteen-sixty-six
Avenue Road Toronto. We were
young, happy in the main if
irked by neighbours overhead
noisy or sneaking our water till
we realised to purchase a padlock
for what we learned to call a faucet...

There a first embryo formed
in me and died self-aborting
agonizingly after we flew
to what had been home in an England
seemed now aging, but not before
kind Doctor Varey would visit
let himself in by a back door
—wouldn't be allowed now
—into our only good-sized
room, the bedroom for which we'd bought
a temporary double spring
thinking after another year
we'd be going—leaving for where?

As would turn out, we would stay
twenty, and four live births
would follow on a second 'miss':
by then another wonder-working
doctor, Jack (as we came to call him)
—his good Irish wit lifting me
out of woe as I narrated
the two 'fails' suffered in England
jesting 'It's the weather there!'

73

he diagnosed the cause: self-same
as the distinguished 'gyne' (and
as I would learn, practitioner
of abortions still illegal)
loudly had ruled out to the
admiring posse of his students
at my bedside, contradicting
correct diagnosis made by
his assistant registrar...

So with diminishing struggle were brought
to the light two sons, between them
a first daughter and last a second:
eyes intellect-bright, hands
translucent, fingers wondrous-gripping
lips that drew a full year on
the breast, determinedly spat out
the proffered foreign teat! How blest
I that had, though now immersed
in other struggle, with the trial
strength to overcome: befriended
by Providence with confidant and
priest, Charles: resting now
in peace, may he pray for us...

But I run on and turn from first
to our second home: old-style
timber-framed its vented gas-heat
made me nervous, but after I'd cleared
rubble from its basement giving
welcome to our first-born. Haply
finding us good tenants, the owner
as autumn set in would provide
double windows for our son's room
and send in Herbie—second novelty:
a real-life Indian!—to paint

and do odd jobs. While warm Fall
days continued our son would sleep
in the second-hand pram we learned
to call a 'buggy', placed in a patch
of garden under a mulberry-tree
shed its sticky berries on him.
Once I recall he lay there bawling
flailing his limbs and you in your
paternity's novelty exclaimed
'I can't stand him when he's like this!'
  . —myself in some desperation
replying, 'Well you'll have to stand him!'
As you did! We went to a lakeside
where, persuaded trepidant
into a boat-ride, I would place
our sleeping son in what I'd learned
to call a closet: fear he'd wake
cry, be kidnapped, ruined the ride!
Photo recalls one of our walks
his coverlet strewn with a first Fall's
glowing tribute of leaves. My son
you had a novice selfish mother
who after our next move—in time
for Christmas and into house now
ours if yet to pay for—returned
to teaching leaving our treasured boy
with a woman seemingly honest
but indolent: a quiet life
her aim. My error you taught me when
she entering one morning as I
fed you breakfast, you at sight of
her convulsed roared your rejection!
Trembling, knowing another child
preparing see the light, I set
myself to mend your desolation.
'Did you not know two years

the worst gap to leave between
births?' intoned another doctor—
female this time. We had homed
again on England little knowing
our war-torn childhoods' cradle
evolving if through setbacks into
case-hardened plutocracy...

Here I leave my little story
being by way of Confession
with the hope their mother will
a little leniency receive
from two and two our sons and daughters
Peter Alice Tom Rebecca

DAY OF ANNUNCIATION 2021

All this dark winter lockdown^
we have clung on listening to The News
of sickness fever death, assessed
experts' discouraging prognoses
avoided friends family strangers
masked up for our daily dole
of recreation rain- or windswept
and darkening as first nights, then
the days raced to outstrip each other:
until today says 'Pause, contemplate
the white-flowering trees beyond
your window, the brown boughs' slow
greening against the white and blue
motion of a Spring-cleaned sky
forsythia goldening below the
dark fence-line while close
to earth odd daffodils nod and
a rare hyacinth rears his head
as if awakening Creation
to greet Annunciation.
                              April
is on his way to wash the tired
leaves green and suddenly God
has set His bow in the heavens: see
arching over our skies in full
pulsating spectrum it stand to tell
sad lonely locked down lackers
of children, friends, of each other
Our anciently guessed as Primavera
Lady is Annunciate again!

---

* In response to the 'Covid' pandemic.

OLD LADIES

Two old ladies our neighbours in
differing neighbourhoods—one
village, one town—both seen
last in care-homes (as they call
those overheated staging-posts
where smiling staff brew up tea
and call you 'Love'—and love it may be!)

I'll call the first Mrs P: don't
think I knew her first name; though
staff there may have used it, that
from me would not have been respectful—
even though she'd become a bit
batty and set fire to her house
giving the Council excuse to evict her.

Mrs W. came later
and I knew her by her first
and classical name Dione.
She was decidedly classical
even though she'd not been
to University. (Mrs P.
had been at the L. S. E.)

Only once in their respective
care-homes did I visit either:
Dione had been diagnosed
with lung-cancer and I forget
what Mrs P. died of; perhaps
I was abroad but I saw neither
again unless you count their coffins.

Now that I'm an old lady
hospital receptionists
and suchlike—not, I think, the doctors
or not yet—call me by my
first name which being that

of some Hebrew ladies gives me
hope old ladies may meet again.

And *a propos* of Hebrew ladies
there was Sophie whom my uncle
married and became Mayor
of Stepney: Sophie in old age
would recall her days of grandeur
in the mayoral coach and though
asthmatic passed her hundredth year:

As has Joyce*—and more; she
inclining to Roman History
and hence Epigraphy became
a World Authority on Inscriptions
Greek and Latin. Her I venture
and have reason to regard
even as a second mother.

Sophie and Joyce would meet upon
wedding of our elder daughter:
only elderly ladies then and
seated in the September sunshine
seems—as the less elder Joyce
recalled it—found a commonalty:
different though one might suppose them . . .

I don't know if such old ladies
as these four persist—I rather
doubt it though they give me hope
I now old myself might follow
in their footsteps, prove myself
of their breed—granting God
and we remaining God's: Amen

---

* Dr Joyce Reynolds died in September 2022 aged 103.

PASSING THOUGHTS

Hark!
Hark!
The music of the rain
pours eases pours again
as it would cleanse else drown
this sullen land alack
centuries adrift
and though rift
narrows yet the wrack
of nations thunders down
on her enfolding shore
while drift we more
from anchorage in home
on tombstone foundations
built for nations
Rome!

FAREWELL

Farewell,
Early-loved sea!
I thank you for the shell
makes relive for me
the lifetime I have sought you
laved in your waves
supped on your scapes
from Cornish cliff Atlantic
(yet blue as the South)
to northern coasts colonized
by kittiwake and gull
by petrel fulmar puffin's
utterance without lull...

LIFE-MAKERS

The things that make my life
the amber glass plates
from Euromarché
and ditto bowl
found by the highway
some picknicker had left
(by now slightly chipped.)
Why do I think of them?
Only that they've endured

DIVERSE QUATRAINS

Purple sky with orange moon
Apocalypse is with us soon.
Orange moon with purple sky
Old continent, you die...

And then they turned on Privilege:
so called they the provision
that those to gain the greatest grades
be those to gain admission.

Dear God, I thank you for my life
and even for those times of strife
when I have fought against you, quailed
and fought again—and You prevailed.

AND FINALLY...
(*A Donne-ish sort of roundel*)

'Give me a humble and a contrite heart'

and turn o God apart
your eye from sins I own
nor 'of youth' alone
nor as a denying age off-begs
as 'guilt complex'
but in Your truth

caught in toils am I
and deserving die
but for Thy ruth!
Beauty that You limbed
by which I levied praise
it is but days
till all be dimmed

and if to love's lure sued
in children of our blood
I'd turn for grace displayed
yet Truth shall need
of gratitude His meed...
Then am I dismayed
but for Thy ruth

and but that in Your eye
itself reflected
unseeing must life die
to loss constricted:
except You day on day
write within this breast
Your servant word

"It is the Lord!
He gives, He takes away
His name be blest."

www.ingramcontent.com/pod-product-compliance
Lightning Source LLC
LaVergne TN
LVHW091204080426
835509LV00006B/820